A NATURAL CURIOSITY

poems by

A C Clarke

Published 2011
by New Voices Press
imprint of the Federation of Writers (Scotland)

www.writersfederation.org.uk

ISBN 978-1-906708-12-2

Cover image by Colin Baird
Cover photograph provided by Professor Tony Payne, University of Glasgow

Acknowledgements

My thanks are due to Professor Tony Payne of Glasgow University for providing the cover image and for permission to use it, to Kona McPhee for excellent advice on some of these poems and her very kind comments on the collection as a whole, and to my fellow Caledonian poets for their suggestions and encouragement.

A C Clarke

Some of these poems have appeared in *Causeway, Fras* and *Poetry News. The anatomists* was a runner-up in the 2009 Robert McLellan poetry awards. *Cyclops* won Stirling Library's 2011 OffTheStanza poetry competition.

The Museum of Anatomy

The Museum of Anatomy at the University of Glasgow is a department of the Hunterian Museum, which first opened in 1807 to display the collections bequeathed to the University by the anatomist and obstetrician William Hunter. It is Scotland's oldest public museum.

The Museum Hall in which Hunter's anatomical specimens are now housed was designed by Sir John James Burnet and opened in 1902. Hunter's specimens and the plaster casts made from the plates of his treatise on the gravid uterus are mainly displayed in the upper gallery alongside specimens from the collection of John Cleland, Regius Professor of Anatomy at the University of Glasgow from 1877 to 1910, which include comparative dissections of animal organs and some human malformations.

My interest in the collections stems from a fascination with the workings both of the human body and the human psyche. The specimens on display here reveal to us the intricate nature of our humanity and at the same time raise disturbing questions. The poems that follow attempt to explore some of the tensions inherent in their difficult subject matter.

A C Clarke

CONTENTS

page

For Gavin

A NATURAL CURIOSITY

Humani nihil a me alienum puto
(Terence, estimated life 195-159 BCE)

1   The Anatomists

Their trophy cases line the walls
of the medical school. Imagine their patience
the deftness with which they'd ease a kidney
free of its moorings, scoop a brain out of its shell
under dull light in a fug of ether and coal-gas
their white coats bloodying like a butcher's.

And in the mounting such attention to detail!
See how they rolled back muscle-sleeves
from a flayed arm before digging to the bone,
assembled exact as Meccano
the twenty-seven bones of a filleted hand
syringed quicksilver through tissue-slivers

until they glowed, starbursts in formalin.
Even a fused foetus, toggled across
its opened chest with stitches no seamstress would own,
displayed for dramatic effect, each head tilted
openmouthed away from the lungs
which couldn't breathe for them both.

All this for a final answer. On the brink
these men could walk blithe among skulls,
bottle stillbirths, with the same cool zeal
their tutor preached, whose corpse (his last request)
his students carved — while noting with precision
the curious pathology of the heart.

2   A natural curiosity

gleams — one would think — from his alert glass eyes.
He props his hooves on the mounting plinth
surprised as anyone to find his torso
split at the chest into two, each poised on its own
hindlegs, a double Bambi at ease in his skin.

A sunflecked forest seems to rise behind him,
where the herd browses, stag on guard,
fawns tugging their dams at the teat,
while he trots out on six elegant limbs
whisking off flies with a twitch of each tail.

3 Misbirths In Bottles

One would be enough
to make the point, whatever
the point is. Two, three —
more — suggests obsessiveness
beyond sanctioned enquiry.

4 Woman In The Hunterian

She's taking details
in a small leather notebook.
A poem? Story?
I see her as a rival
then see myself as petty.

5 Hearts In Bottles

These hearts seem chosen
for their history — human
not medical. Stray
accidents sabotaged them
if we trust labels.

6   Honeymooner's Heart

His old man's heart beat high the day
her father led her down the aisle, the bride
he'd fixed on months ago. She stood at his side
in her maid's white, pledged herself away.
He could scarcely hear her voice, his own
a stammer. When he slipped the ring
on her fourth finger his pulse was racing.
Her hand felt cold.
                     As they walked back down
the length of the church, one flesh, he leaned
on her arm. Her lips smiled, but she turned her face
away. At the wedding feast men spoke
their good luck wishes. He thanked them. Longed
for them to leave. She lay in his embrace
that night. His heart rose, brimming. Broke.

7   Heart Pierced By A Chisel

The evidence is here.
The flesh is flesh indeed, the chisel steel.
They look made for each other.

I feel my own heart wince.
That huge splinter driving in!
How could his carpenter's hand

so quick, so deft, have slipped?
The point stabbed home with spearthrust force
left him transfixed.

8 Expectations

It's raining the day she gets the letter
she's been expecting. Expecting!
There's more than one meaning. It
strikes cold to her stomach. She
doesn't need to think, hurries on her
goloshes, stumbles out into the wet
streets, almost running, so that
people stare. Her long dark hair is
shaking loose from its bun, her face is
streaked with water, she hasn't even
stopped to put on her pelisse. Her
fingers fumble the clasp of the
reticule as she rummages for her
purse. The apothecary hands over
the package, doesn't ask questions.
For mice, she'd said. Back home she
shakes the powder into a glass, stirs it
briskly in milk. Three deep breaths
and *Here's to you and me* she says as
she drinks the last toast, one hand on
her belly. She hadn't expected it
would be so painful or take so long.
She has time to wish it undone, as
she'd wished undone that night when
a summer moon and a glass too many
had started the new life her lover had
promised so often. New life! For
sure there's more meanings than one.

9 **Organ In Bottle**

Stomach, this one. Dark-
stained, eroded, rather small
for a woman. Shrunk
by poison like the liver
of an impenitent drunk.

10 **Couple In The Hunterian**

This young couple pause
by a display of things gone
wrong. Would one of them prefer
to be elsewhere? They move on,
his hand on her arm, steering her.

11 Upper Gallery, Anatomy Museum 1

Preserved for posterity, the sell-by-date
centuries off, these singular pickles
will outlive any store-cupboard chutney.

The fluid they're bathing in has puffed them out
to yellow pudginess, flesh become dough.

Don't think you're looking at a severed prick,
a foetal puppy, a seven-month embryo —
for that's the trick of it. It's why

the students here can turn their backs,
hands tap, tap, tapping, eyes searching the screens.

Technicians flick switches to help me see.
I switch lights off, blood mounting my cheeks,
and drop my eyes, like one accused.

12 Girl In The Upper Gallery

Perhaps she was late
and, seats already taken,
had to sit on her own.
Perhaps, like me, she chooses
the comfort of being alone.

13 Students In The Upper Gallery

They are flesh and blood.
They have a right to be here —
more than I perhaps.
Their busy hands will be warm,
pink-flushed. I am glad of that.

14 Upper Gallery, Anatomy Museum 2

As in an over-full Victorian parlour
where flowers and fruit wax eloquent
under their extinguishing covers
(the small bird sucked of its breath in the flare
of candles, all eyes focused)
ornate, unusable objects are peered at
through glass that will always look dusty,
although the things themselves appear to float
in liquid gaslight which gives them the weird
clarity of a sketch by Aubrey Beardsley.

Victorian parlour's only half the story:
dead-eyed trout, robins stiff on their perches,
tinted photographs of babies
too pale to be asleep — that industry
of keepsakes and reanimations —
though they'd catch something of the feel
of this display couldn't match it for brio.
You'd have to dive beyond the reach of day
among wrecks framed in barnacles
sea cucumbers waving pallid tentacles

polyps that glow in the dark
to find such disregard for the proprieties,
and such inventiveness. The multiforms
that stow inside our skeletons
reveal themselves in all their bulge and coil
unlikely as a giant squid, spendthrift in sheer
diversity, from corrugated brain
to swelling liver. You can't tell healthy from sick,
inspect these entrails in a blear
between wonder and nightmare.

15 Joseph Wright's Painting

Air-pump experiment.
It's the little girls who hide
their eyes, who shed tears
for a bird proving a point.
The painting is not about them.

16 Victorian Parlour

Glass domes over wax
flowers, to prevent dustfalls
(dust falls, fine-sifted,
on glass, on glassed-in petals) —
they are lies, like embalming.

17 Stills

Those babies in their shawls
for christenings that wouldn't happen
did they bring comfort?
Like choosing a careful name
to chisel on a stone
shaped like a child's soft toy.

18 Creator

He takes a mix of lime and sand,
shapes cold bellies big with child,

sectioned wombs
in which the unborn hang like fruit.

The casts harden, their contours round
as polished stone. They become

goddess torsos dug from a seabed,
bambini asleep in sculpted cradles.

He can't leave it there, paints them rust-red.
like orlop decks painted that colour

so sailors couldn't see how life
was spilling from their breached bodies.

19 Three Of A Kind

What are these three doing here?
They look of an age
to be viable, just.
They are not curled
for the tight fit of the womb.
Their mouths are open.
I'd say they'd made it
to air. Pot-bellied,
heavy-headed, as is the nature
of those born early,
nothing at first sight
seems to be missing,
nothing messed up.
Three in a row
in a dance routine
spindle bow legs
spindle arms akimbo
singing a tune
which is never going to change.

20 **Double Take**

See here a toddler's arm,
the plump wrist creased,
the dimpled fingers curving

as if waiting for the mother
to clasp all six tight in her own.
Hush now, she'd say, *it's all right.*

There in the next jar, harshly lit,
hangs another, the mirror image
down to its *supernumerary digit.*

Whoever labelled them typed neatly
on old-fashioned keys, their medic's language
precise. No sign of a slip.

What I'm looking at spelled out.
Twice over. Still I fail to grasp.

21 Cyclops

Little turnip-face
hung in this jar like a jack o'lantern
you turn your botched eye
to the staring world.

There's something in the quirk
of your hobgoblin mouth
that seems to mock
yet might break into sobs
any moment.

Little changeling
you are so other
and so human.

They wouldn't show you to your mother.
I wish she could have held you,
stroked your auburn curls,
traced the whorls
of your delicate, perfect ears.

---

[1] *Medical term for a rare deformity in which a foetus is born with the eyes fused in the centre of the forehead.*

22 Upper Gallery, Anatomy Museum 3

A junk shop, almost.
Lemur, tiger, shark (parts
of them) jostle
human organs, whole, diseased,
plaster casts of pregnant wombs

accumulated clutter
which no-one is going to buy
but anyone can view
to while away an hour
between meeting and meeting.

23 Night In The Anatomy Museum

As if a watercolour by some demented
Victorian botanist had walked off the page
into a bottle, the mauvish stem

of a windpipe flexes its coils,
branches, buds downward,
each lung-lily opening in the liquid

which holds it on the verge
of breath alongside a whole gallery
of body-blooms on best behaviour.

But when the lights are out and the door locked
the slippery flowerheads fill and sigh
in the funnelled breeze, the long stem pulses,
deepens to purple, purple
the lobes of the lilies as they flush,
pale, flush, drumming the glass
in a one-two beat — it's catchy — the blanched stalk
of a neighbour larynx undulates to the rhythm,
a snapdragon heart close by
swings on its hinges open and shut,
while in the facing showcase
a tiger's tongue — great spotted orchid —
unfurls, searches its trap for missing parts,
yowls soundless, severed from the root.

24 Aesthetics

Beardsley, botanists' sketches:
the body's artwork,
fluid, fluent, holds
its own beauty if we get
beyond our natural tremor

at seeing ourselves
inside out. For 'all that lives
is holy' — I would say
all that lives has found
the shape to be itself.

25 Sections of tissue

seem like harps or lyres
draped in translucent scarlet-fading-to-pink.
What spectral fingers pluck their feathery strings?

What music beyond human range
sings the body's subcutaneous deeps,
the caves where mineral riches grow

layer on layer until a delving scalpel
lifts to the surface fibrin masterworks
whose folds outpleat an origami rose?

26 **Patterns**

Capillaries of
heart and lungs divide then sub-
divide: branches, twigs

bladderwrack sacs
bubble like alveoli
filling up with air

water flows into
intricate busy deltas
a map of blue veins

hand, fingers splayed
sycamore leaf, ridged ribs
like metacarpals

the bee's honeycomb eye
probing the hive, galaxies
coiled in a thumbprint

27 **Section Of Bone**

Stick of rock: cut it across
the stamped-in script is readable
down to the last sliver

Finely reticulate, a crochet net
in calcium, more delicate
than cobwebs, stronger

The massed pipes of a mini-organ
tuned to bat-squeak, lacework scrimshaw

Giant's Causeway in Lilliput
fossil honeycomb, frozen Aero

28 Last Exhibits

Drawn to the human
as to a mirror image
I pause in front of people in
various stages of undress,
down to the last

layer. I want to say
'Although you are bone-naked
I imagine you
in crinoline or frock-coat —
whatever garb you wore

in your time. Your voice
might fall strangely on these ears
tuned to the present.
Let me extend my hand to yours
though between us is glass.'

29 Penal

The basic principle I use for my decisions is this: guilt is always beyond a doubt.
(From *In The Penal Colony* by Franz Kafka)

Skeletons can be read
the way a policeman
reads his notebook.
An evening in a brothel
dented this browbone
a lifetime's pipe-smoking
wore down those molars.

Don't think you've lived blameless.
Your father's whore
cratered your shinbones
your sunless childhood
bandied your legs
those years you stitched in an attic
have twisted your tubercular spine.

Nature's a stern judge —
nothing personal.
You may not recognise your crimes.
Those who exhume
what you melt down to
will find the human record
through and through.

30 Missing

Everything is here.
DIY kit for a latter-day Frankenstein.
Devices for every function,
plumbing more intricate
than a boiler-room,
electric circuits faster
than a PC.
Blueprints for respiration,
digestion, gender.
Nowhere among these bottled wonders,
not even in the softroe folds of the brain,
a thought winged mid-flight
in all its fiery plumage.

31 **Head Of Cadaver**
dissected to show the superficial temporal artery

Half of the skin has been cut away
on the left side of the neck; but it's his face

that makes me look again. The tucks at the lips
hint at teeth gone, yet a firmness

in the mouth's upward curve — no rictus —
bespeaks a measured kindliness.

Stitched shut, the papery brown lids
are calm as sleep. He has made sanctuary

among these displaced body parts,
a saint in some Old Master's repertory

of martyrdom, who, skinned to his tubes,
smiles; gives blessing.

BIOGRAPHICAL NOTE

A C Clarke, an active member of Scottish PEN, moved to Glasgow from London in 2002. She has been widely published in magazines and competition anthologies and has won a number of poetry competitions, most recently the Grey Hen competition and the Stirling OffTheStanza poetry competition. Her pamphlet *The Gallery on the Left* was published by Akros in 2003, and her first full collection *Breathing Each Other In* by Blinking Eye Publishers in 2005, followed by *Messages of Change* by Oversteps Books in 2008. Her third full collection, *Fr Meslier's Confession*, is due out from Oversteps Books early in 2012. She was Makar of the Federation of Writers (Scotland) from 2007 to 2008.

New Voices Press
2011